A World without Money or Politicians

By

Colin Walpole

Dedication

To an Indian woman, a Brazilian boy, a spirit and a hedge fund manager.

Table of Contents

Contents

A World without Money or Politicians

By Colin Walpole

Introduction

It has taken about seven years to put this piece together and you will find some notes along the way that indicate a date when something happened that influenced my thoughts. It might be something I read or a video I saw, I hope this does not spoil the reading experience, but it is not exactly 'War and Peace', so please be patient. A booklet of this type is not the modern way to spread an idea, nevertheless I feel comfortable with this format. It is honest and I feel that I can stand accountable for the things written here.

The one fact of life that I cannot ignore is *'might beats right'* and I have no might. One voice outside the established political arena will have little effect, but there are murmurings abroad that match the arguments made here. Everyone should have a little might whether they be right or wrong and no one person or group should have it all.

A warning before you read on – I recommend a form of governance which is a coming together of communism and democracy. Please do not prejudge. Read with an open mind, it is an open mind that has written it.

My radical conclusions surprise me even now and I hope, as a by-product, this document will help explain them. If I have been radicalised (the buzzword at the moment), it has not been by some sinister third party. My lifetime experiences and keen observation have led me to this place. I have written this totally independently, and often in the face of a strong head wind, so conspiracy theorists need look no further. The media, thought by some to be a source of systematic brain washing, seems to have had the reverse effect on me. TV, newspapers and, more recently, social media is the lens through which I see the world.

I have always taken an interest in current affairs but have never been politically engaged and I have certainly never been a member of any political party. A busy family life, working in order to keep the wolf from the door left no surplus capacity to harbour ambitions of 'social reform'.

I am an Englishman living in Denmark and although the prescribed system outlined here points towards it being implemented in the UK, it could be adapted anywhere. If someone, somewhere in the world is inspired by reading this, please feel free to expand on it and let the idea grow. But use it peacefully, change does not come easily, I hope no one takes the thoughts laid down here and uses violence to impose them on any existing regime.

***

This small journal advocates two immense changes to our culture and philosophy. The changes are for the benefit of the planet and all of its inhabitants, especially mankind.

They are –

1. The abolition of money and the dismantling of the economy.
2. To make all career politicians redundant and change from representative democracy to direct democracy.

I am not exactly sure when this notion of a moneyless society first struck me, there was no 'Damascus road experience', but over the last eighteen years or so, I have convinced myself that money and economics stand in the way of individual self-fulfilment (I have a whole list of grievances targeted at the dominance of the economy over all else, but I will focus here on individual self-fulfilment). About ten years ago and inspired by these thoughts I started to write 'The Lives and Deaths of Terry Toft' a story about a futuristic moneyless society. The protagonist is small boy born in 2269, who has previously lived during current times and has his memory of that life intact. I found it liberating to let my imagination loose in a novel, but I have shifted to this more direct and provocative format. I will get around to finishing Terry Toft one day. However, it would be interesting to travel forward in time and delve into the archives of 2269 that cover our current period. This little contribution would most likely be lost together with a whole stack of protest songs. But I feel the people of 2269 would nevertheless conclude that money was barbaric and that politicians were superfluous – assuming of course that there is a world in 2269.

The idea of a moneyless society is not new, of course, I was reminded of that recently when I thought a blog might be a good way of generating feedback. Googling first 'how to blog' and then 'blogs about moneyless societies' identified some examples: the Venus Project – Jacque Fresco and the Moneyless Man – Mark Boyle were prominent. I progressed no further in this 'blog' direction, a mist appeared and the techno barrier that plagues me descended.

Money steals our freedom

I love the sweet taste of sugar and, in my younger days, I loved the way a good India Pale Ale hit my palate and I love money. We all love money. I am even guilty of buying an occasional lottery ticket in the hope of enjoying a retirement without the fear of my small pension pot expiring before I do. As life progresses, you adjust your diet to appease metabolic shifts, changes have to be made. Your outlook on life changes, too, and then, out of the blue, you discover that your life-long focus has been misdirected – the target of your vision shrinks – you realise that it was a mirage.

At a young age, we learn about money and that is when the pursuit for it begins. That pursuit is most often powered by a formal education followed by a career when the money starts rolling in. But that is not always the path. In a modern society like ours, you need money – so you work for it, perhaps you inherit some, or maybe the state supports you – or a combination of these. If a sound education is not available or if there are no jobs, a life of crime may be the only source of income. Either way, you cannot ignore money, it is the key to everything material and, to those who seek power, money is the ultimate lever. The less money you have, or the more you want, dictates the activity levels necessary to maintain a healthy income. While you wrestle with this distraction, life is passing you by.

Money dictates our behaviour

Those who are poor or live under financial stress are weighed down by the worry of making ends meet – they think almost exclusively of money whereas the wealthy can take a more relaxed view of life and enjoy the freedom of letting their thoughts dwell on finer things. In a world without money, this freedom would be available to all.

Money, I believe, has outlived its usefulness; it has fulfilled its purpose, transported man and the planet to current times and is now redundant. No longer is it a mere token to be used as an exchange for goods, money is an established commodity like any other and is traded on international markets like crude oil, rice or corn. And nowadays governments print money and feed it into the economy via quantitative easing.

Maybe history will show that the most significant progress of our time is not machines and artificial intelligence taking over jobs, but the slow death of money and the economy. I fear that without any conscious effort to manage its decline as suggested here, the boom-and-bust cycle will continue to spin out of control like a dollop of off-centre clay on a potter's wheel. As with the ageing family dog or the overgrown tree in the small suburban garden, difficult decisions have to be made.

At my school, there were things that were taught and things that were learnt. Charlton Secondary School for Boys did not train its pupils in macroeconomics. Nor did it teach us how to deal with bullies – that was something that had to be learnt the hard way –and more serious disputes were sorted out in the park across the road after school. We were taught all the general academic things, maths and English, etc. as well as technical drawing, woodwork, metalwork and, critically for me, rugby.

We observed that some boys were not like the rest of us and these were treated with respect, any teasing was quickly snuffed out. We learnt from each other the survival skills of South East London. I left in 1964, aged 16, with a few 'O'-levels and a handful of CSE-passes of unremarkable grades. Had Harrow or Eton been my source of education, I probably would not be writing this.

I was never looking for arguments for my cause – I had no cause – it emerged naturally from the following and similar:

The Indian woman living with her children in cardboard boxes on the central reservation of a dual carriageway in Calcutta.

The Brazilian boy whose lungs were destroyed by smoke from printed circuits recovered from a scrap heap of European computers and burned to recover precious metals.

The Indian baby left to die in an incubator, because his or her parents could not afford the cost of the electricity to run it. (India has a space programme, bear in mind).

The American hedge fund manager with his seven New York apartments and five helicopters.

My feelings of sympathy go equally to the American investor, since he is perhaps more lost and deluded than those affected by poverty.

These are newsworthy examples (of which there are thousands) that pop up frequently, but each of us has our own story to tell of skirmishes caused by money or the lack of it.

Then there is my beloved Rugby Union. Once proudly an amateur sport, it has now turned professional and players pump iron all day in order to become bigger and stronger, scrums do not work, because the ratio between muscle mass and the soles of their boots is no longer proportionate. Wealthy men buy clubs and exercise their egos by buying the best players. Needless to say, it is the same in football and all professional sports. The real competition is the bulging company cheque book.

In the recent scandal concerning FIFA, the bribes and corruption were only picked up by US prosecutors because, it seems, bribes do not attract tax. What exactly distinguishes normal business practice from corruption?

You do not need money to play football, you need a ball. When we were kids, we played football on 'The Point' in Greenwich, a part of Blackheath. We played for hours with boys coming and going, no adults, no whistle, no goal posts, no pitch markings and no referee. There were disputes and fights, but we sorted it out and the game continued. How lucky I was to have this as part of my development. It was not until years later whilst visiting 'The Point' with my small son Alex that I noticed grass now growing where we had once played football – back then, it never had a chance to grow.

Look at cycling. The desire for success turned a sport into a competition for pharmacists. I understand competiveness, I understand the will to win, but a sportsperson's top achievement should not be drug-assisted.

There are, of course, many examples of inequality in the distribution of wealth and you may argue that there are less radical ways to address this than abolishing money. But my point goes beyond the arbitrary nature of the distribution of wealth. It is the domination of the economy over everything else. Money and the balancing of the books are prioritised over both human needs and the well-being of our planet. I believe that this will continue to be the case as long as money exists. Reflect on your own life and the way it has been moulded by money and the economy. Look closely at your actions over recent times. How many of your activities were dictated by money and how much time did you set aside for yourself and those close to you? Even if you are comfortably off or privileged, you may find yourself worried about your investments or the interest rates. You may even question the true motives of future sons – or daughters-in-law. Gold will always attract gold-diggers.

An example of how the dominance of money dehumanises us is illustrated by the well-publicised case of the American car manufacturer who, on discovering a design fault in a popular family car – a rear-end shunt would cause the petrol tank to explode – opted not to disrupt production by changing the design. It would have been too costly, deadlines would not be met and competition with Japanese manufacturers would be negatively affected. It was cheaper to pay compensation to the families roasted alive in the accidents. Business is business.

In my case, the sugar and the India Pale Ale had to go – for the sake of society at large and the environment, money has to go.

After debating my ideas with a friend, he sent me a pamphlet from the 1970s issued by the Communist Party. I read it with great disappointment, expecting a light-bulb moment, but none came, *'perhaps I was truly a communist and I could join the communist party and live happily ever after'*. The contents of the pamphlet were short-sighted, and between the lines I could only see indulgent, chip-on-shoulder side swipes aimed at the ruling classes. It seemed British communists of that era had an interest in preserving the class system instead of breaking it down. In the world as I imagine it, there will be no class – as you will read later. My friend may have seen me as a closet communist, using the pamphlet to tease me out. You may also see me as a communist and perhaps I am, in part, but I believe the irresistible urge of categorising each other in this way is yet another cop-out, it obscures complexities that are worth closer examination. And to defend the 'working classes' is to condone the idea that the class concept is legitimate. It isn't.

When I left school aged 16, I started an apprenticeship to become a motor mechanic and, after the first year, changed to auto electrician (fixing car electrics, less mucky). I learnt the skill of fault-finding. If a fuse blew, you had to find out why, and this meant tracing the circuits of colour-coded wiring – sometimes the whole length the car – looking for signs of chaffing or some other damage. Ears and nose were used on occasions when the cables disappeared into the chassis, and you would sometimes smell burning or hear the wires shorting where they rubbed on a sharp piece of metal. It is no good changing the fuse until you have found the fault.

I am not an angry man, but take the case of the Brazilian boy – it was a TV documentary – I recall my reaction, I was livid, my eyes were burning and I wanted to help. How could I help? Send money? The little chap was working to earn money for his family, he was proud and pragmatic about his achievements, but his lungs were permanently damaged. If I sent money it might help him, but other children would only take his place. Money was the fault – not the solution. When I trace the circuits using the examples listed above, I find the fault to be the existence of money. While money exists, there will be those who have lots and those who have little or none. Open your daily newspaper, apply the fault-finding exercise to the articles you read and, in about half of the cases, you will find that it is money or the economy that is 'blowing the fuse'.

My upbringing in Greenwich just after the war taught me fair play. My rugby career (distinct only by its longevity) taught me fair play. Roy Rogers and Hop-Along Cassidy on black and white television taught me fair play. It is not fair that people have to suffer because of poverty when the prime cause of poverty is money.

I accept that it is an unjust and unfair world, sickness, accidents and natural disasters occur routinely and my standpoint is prone to easy criticism of naivety. A reader may not detect it here, but I am very self-critical, cautious and often full of self-doubt; nevertheless I believe wholly in the arguments that I present here.

This is how it has been since the industrial revolution (also before, but less so) -;

An entrepreneur takes some raw material and, using a work force, non-renewable energy and some ingenuity he/she creates a product which is sold at a profit. The workers are paid and so have a disposable income.

This process has been replicated over and over for generations and now we have a complex and inter-dependable commercial world, we have consumers and the whole thing works because of money. And what's wrong with that?

This process (consumerism) is killing the planet – that is what is wrong with it.

Advertising drives consumerism. Jobs have to be found even though machines and artificial intelligence have reduced the need for workers (computers don't spend money). This should be good news but, instead of a shorter working week, employees are laid off and pushed into stressful circumstances and humiliation. They have been encouraged to borrow money and now they have no job and no income to repay their loans – that is what's wrong with it.

The workhouse, the poor law, debtor's prison, depressions, inflation, deflation, quantitative easing, boom and bust, repossessions, ivory, deforestation and tragically sad suicides – all of these are answers to the question 'and what's wrong with that?' (Please feel free to add to this list).

Economics is a lie, a pseudo-science

Economics is man-made. It is a lie that benefits a few superficially but no one in the long term. Although as a subject it rubs shoulders with physics and chemistry, a more appropriate bedfellow would be astrology.

Take the charity that shows the school built with monies collected. An impoverished African location is the setting and a child being interviewed expresses his ambition to be an engineer or a doctor, you recognise the scenario, I know the intentions are honourable, but the school is only producing more money users, more tax payers and the poor lad will probably never achieve those ambitions no matter how hard he works. I am not saying 'do not support charities'; under the current regime, it is the only way to help. What I am saying is 'change your thinking'. Look at your life, look at the ones you love, look at your neighbours and your local environment and try to imagine life without money and the constant nag of the economy.

November 2016 – the autumn budget. We should not have to llsten lu so-called economic experts commenting on 'Office for Budget Responsibility' forecasts as if they were factual. Merely discussing the matter on TV bestows unwarranted credence, confusing unwary viewers as opinions come across as facts. These forecasts are invariably inaccurate, but can be alarming when delivered, there will be no statements two or five years hence apologising for misleading the public. The forecasters and the journalists are fantasists who, when the end of money is realised, can happily make the transition to become writers of fairy tales.

Part 2 - POLITICS

Politics can be baffling. The first political happening that I did not understand was the war (World War II), if war can be described as a political happening. I was born in 1948 so it is through the eyes of a child that I recall this. The war made people cry, adults that is. You may agree that it is very upsetting for children to see adults crying for no apparent reason – they have not fallen and grazed their knee, so why cry?

My generation was lucky with its grown-ups. Looking back, I can see that the war had given them a special perspective on life. One way or another, everyone mourned, not just for those close to them, but also for the unknown, the remote, the victims of the holocaust and, I suppose, the mourning was accompanied by a sense of the utter waste of lives and simple stupidity of war. Some of the tears may even have been shed for the shame of being part of it, of the initial pride of seeing their young men marching off to war. Their crying was like the cow's hopeless calling for her stolen calf. They had been duped.

Perhaps I was lucky, these grown-ups loved their children and the children around them, my teachers were dutiful and respectful of their charges, aware of the solemn responsibility they owed to the unspoilt and untarnished. That is how it seemed to me then and, although I was only four of five, I can see that I was right, confused but right, no power, no smart articulation, no might – but right.

A basic education cannot teach us everything – sometimes it is wise to ask a child. Growing up in Greenwich during this period was my first view of life. Children never read newspapers, we had no TV, the Bakelite radio delivered 'Mrs Dale's Diary' and 'the

Archers' and us kids would enjoy 'Listen with Mother'.

Since those days in the fifties, many political events have occurred and I will not begin to list them here. But listen to children and to the voice of old soldiers – then listen to your politicians.

*

Jobs and work fill a big part of this re-think. Imagine the chancellor's build-up to an election 'build more houses, improve road and rail links, create new jobs'.

'Growth', the holy grail of the economy has to stop, it has to shrink and then reverse. We can't just carry on building. Nor should we launch vacuous projects simply in order to feed the economy. Properties stand empty, properties owned by investors, property bonds and pension funds. Homes should mean homes.

(Just watched Phil Collins's 'Just another Day in Paradise' 100 million homeless in the world. This is a powerful song and a moving video highlighting homelessness and poverty. Difficult to see any suggestion of a solution, but throwing money at the problem is not the way. Again, money is the problem. There are homes and food enough. Of course, if I sent Phil Collins details of my thoughts, he might be alarmed – perhaps his perception of himself is marked by his financial success and the removal of his wealth might scare him. But that is the way we are programmed to think. His real wealth is his creativity, which will live on, long after his money is spent.)

Another thing that made my heart sink was a headline I saw recently: 'Care is costing millions'. Care!

Care vb. – to be worried or concerned, to like or be fond of. (Collins English Dictionary).

Over the generations, marketing has evolved so that everything can be packaged and priced – but care?

At the mention of communism, one immediately thinks of cruel dictators and enforced uniformity. The communism detailed here isn't like that. There are no dictators and there is no pyramid of government.

Under this new thinking, there is no left, right or centre politics – all of that is gone. Questions or proposals are put to the people for the people to decide. Why should we be forced to choose between sets of unreliable parties who, in turn, are forced to make fanciful promises in order to gain power?

Gone will be the thespian gaze into a distant horizon, gone the measured pause, the spin and the posing. And why will that be gone? Because there is no power struggle – critically, power has been moved to its rightful place in the lap of those responsible for voting (listed later). The system of governance proposed here is a true marriage of democracy and communism, most importantly, it cuts out the middleman, the career politician.

'Should there be a new railway link between London and the North?' Ask the people! People are not daft, they know it is not necessary, that it is just another job creating scheme, jobs that are temporary, of course, a project that is a disaster for the environment but excusable (desirable even) under the current regime.

Within the new regime outlined here, *you* will have the power to act in order to invoke change. If, for example, you think density of population is important, you can raise the issue by putting a question to parliament. You do not have to find a party to do that, and if there are enough people who think that density of population is a factor that affects quality of life, it can be debated and policies set in place – or not. The outcome is not tainted by money, there are no backhanders for building contracts; the central issue here is the welfare of the people, not profit.

(We are currently – April 2015 – in the run up to an election – there is no attempt by the political parties to disguise their shameful lust for power).

(And now – November 2016 – with Trump president elect. What has this circus to do with humanity? How can it be that one person can have so much power over so many?)

So far, I have suggested a society without money and without politicians, a world where the well-being of the planet and all of its inhabitants tops the agenda. The outcome of these changes will result in the opportunity for every man, woman and child to live a fulfilled life.

Why will that be the result? There are, of course, many fulfilled people in the world. Professional sports men and women, top musicians and entertainers, for example. But on close examination, and sadly this examination will often be an obituary, their private lives often seem tragically unhappy. Rags-to-riches stories frequently show journeys plagued by wealth spent on drugs and self-destruction. We often see this incongruous picture of our heroes only when they are no more. Instead of being well-balanced, many have spent a career – twisting, contorting and jumping through hoops in order to please.

And, of course, not all fulfilled people are famous, there are many who find fulfilment within their work and hobbies. Parenting and other close relationships provide fulfilment, too.

We should have all the time we need to explore our creativity. Painting, writing and art in all its forms, sport, fitness and looking after our minds and bodies are critical. If we don't do this, if we don't spend time, alone or in groups, finding out about ourselves and each other, then a great part of our personality and therefore humanity, remains uncharted. This is a process that should start at an early age and never cease. We should all be pushing boundaries and trying new things throughout our lives.

Instead of 'career advice', or 'my son is going to follow in my footsteps' or 'my daughter is going to be this or that'. The stress should be on who the person 'is' and not what he or she is 'going to be'. Establishing a person's abilities, preferences and characteristics at a young age should be standard procedure, not the exception.

There is even a perverse fulfilment in simply surviving in a world that is limiting and ill-fitting. Shortly after beginning my apprenticeship, I found that it was a job to which I was totally unsuited. I had two left hands and ten thumbs and it took ages to learn which way to turn a nut to undo it. I practised at home with a nut and a bolt and my Micky Mouse wristwatch, but then one day, underneath a filthy meat lorry with the stench of rotten mutton churning my stomach and plump maggots falling onto oil soaked sawdust, the bolt I had to remove was pointing away from me, meaning the reverse was now true and my newly learned skills had to be re-jigged. Rusty U-bolts holding layers of suspension springs covered in grease and road dirt had to be dismantled. Puny hands reaching up, the blood and strength draining, add to that the fear of the axle stands giving way, (not unheard of) and being crushed to death, this 16-year-old pined for his childhood. I would love to end this anecdote by recalling a stiffening of sinew and summoning of blood, but the truth was some tough love from my parents who sent me off to work again the next day.

What a misuse of five years. I managed to live as an auto-electrician for a further fifteen years after which I was recruited into the life assurance industry, selling life assurance, pensions, mortgages and investments – another square hole. And it continues, now I'm a gravedigger in Denmark!

(Retired October 2016).

There are other more dramatic examples of people walking the wrong path. The boxing promoter who, late in life, had the courage to change sex. He had never felt comfortable in a male body, but lived a life in the macho world of boxing. He was very successful, but at what price did that success come?

If we cannot be ourselves – if people live the wrong lives – what effect does that have on society as well as on individuals? I know these things are not always directly attributable to money, but my point is that the obsession with money (not particularly greed for money, but the fact that, under the current regime, we need it to live) reduces the chances of us following passions and paths of curiosity that might lead to a more meaningful existence.

Perhaps you suddenly realised as a child that you did not fit in. Perhaps you blushed, your eyes filled and you melted away to re-invent yourself. No one noticed and you meet again having severed a whole part of your personality, maybe forever or maybe for it to fester only to reappear later in a dwarfed form. We are all full of ourselves from time to time and having the rough edges knocked off makes us into more rounded characters, and that is not what I mean. It is the unarticulated assumption that we conform, that we do not point and laugh at the emperor's new suit of clothes.

An example of this is the strangulating effect of political correctness on freedom of speech.

As we mature, we naturally develop, we outgrow our skins, we learn from our mistakes and look back thankfully at the tolerance of those around us. In turn, we should learn to forgive the demeanours of others and support the next generation through their mistakes.

It would be a strange child who, when asked what they would like to be when they grew up, answered 'me'. But a wise child, too. I have even seen – it was an advert on TV – a mother asking a daughter '*who* would you like to be when you grow up? i.e. 'What other person would you like to be?' They were actors, of course, and no one is going to suffer directly from this one advert, but it goes to make up the whole distortion of the world as we, and especially young people, see it and relate it to themselves. I object, as you may have gathered by now, to adverts because of their role in the process of consumerism but there are other, more sinister, undertones in the implication that 'if you don't like yourself – be someone else'.

Let me expand on the philosophy of individual fulfilment, because it's critical in understanding the whole idea.

I am uncertain about the existence of God, but persuaded by much of the wisdom passed on from the mainstream religions. In the Bible, there's something about humans being created in the image of God. I buy that concept. Everyone is born pure. When we come into this world, we possess potential that is rarely allowed to develop. One reason for this is poverty. Poor parents often miss out on education and the development of their offspring can be stunted because of lack of support and the peace of mind necessary for them to focus on anything other than survival. In the third world, this may be stark due to lack of food and clean water, war or even the baby's gender. In the UK, it may be more subtle and due to financial pressure, unemployment and even something like having to buy a second- hand pram. All of these things can unsettle a vulnerable mother whose hormones are out of kilter. In many cases, essential elements for the baby's welfare such as eye contact or a lullaby are low on the agenda.

The wealthy do not have it easy either. Their babies may get the eye contact and the lullabies, but as toddlers they are stuffed into prep school uniforms and constantly monitored for signs of genius. And if these signs are absent, the child picks ups signals of disappointment from the parents.

Another reason we rarely fulfil our potential is the track that starts with our upbringing and education; this track leads those that follow it faithfully to a lifetime of work – which earns them money – used to consume goods – and qualifies them to borrow from the bank in order to buy more.

The track that we should be following is our own development, not in an egoistic self-absorbed way but as a challenge to find our limits.

Fulfilment means a baby, a toddler, a child, adolescent, teenager, adult and senior citizen living a life true to his or her self, uninhibited by external expectations but with consideration for the environment and with compassion and respect for his or her fellow humans.

The class system in the UK is particular to the UK, so I will not delve too much into that, but I was classified during my early education as being working class, not particularly academic, and my education was set on a predetermined track. I do not cry 'unfair' - I had a happy childhood and perhaps the lessons that I learned on the streets of Greenwich with bomb sites as playgrounds served me equally as well as a finer education would have done.

When Chris (my son) was small and I would get ready to go to work, he would plead for me not to go. He would pull my face to look at him and say 'just don't go' as if it was that simple. Of course, I had to go to work to earn money and, on explaining this, he would retort 'but just use the hole in the wall, I'll come with you!' And one might detect the same puerile simplicity in my suggestion to abolish money, 'just get rid of it', but please read on.

To understand all of this, one has to be open to the concept that mankind has a special place on this planet. Any reader of this piece may be excused for shrugging their shoulders and concluding that 'money is here to stay, nor will you ever get rid of politicians'.

Man created money – man has to abolish it. The way we organise our day-to-day living is up us, it is up to you.

***

I have analysed in my own way - 'Money and Economics' - 'Politics' - 'Individual Fulfilment'.

This section suggests a system that would realign some of the inequities outlined above.

Aims

1. To dismantle the economy and proceed without money.
2. To replace representative democracy with a hybrid version of direct democracy, a system of parliamentary debate followed by online voting by a section of the population.
3. To build a path to a society where the individual is fulfilled and free – where

we care for each other and the environment.

Order of consideration

1 The planet.

2 All of humanity.

3 Those we share the planet with i.e. plants and the animal kingdom.

***

I outline here (a rough sketch) an alternative form of governance where policies are debated according to the following procedure:

*

The advocate (anyone) formulates the proposal to be debated and submits it to a 'Backing List' where it needs to attract a following sufficient for it to be taken on to the next stage. Qualifying proposals are published so as to give opponents time to formulate a campaign. (Minor items such as new changing rooms at the sports centre will be dealt with locally).

An agreed version of the proposal is then broadcast. Next, the case is debated simultaneously in parliamentary events around the country with evidence produced by both sides. This is similar to the current system, but instead of one debate (at Westminster) there are several. The passion, humour and drama will be harnessed to produce the most sensible outcome with respect for the planet, the people and the environment.

Who? – What is parliament? How is parliament structured? Who participates in the debate? Who chairs, conducts and records proceedings? Who votes?

Each parliamentary debating event is overseen by a chairman and four assistants. These people are periodically changed, but drawn from a spread of different walks of life. (You have to bear in mind that there are no paid jobs because there is no money. When policy is debated, self-interest is restricted to personal leanings and individual wisdom - not financial gain).

Once the initial debating is over, the chairman and his assistants analyse the exchanges and present this analysis in written form, stripped of theatre and hyperbole. Too much of current politics is distorted by personality rather than the merits of the argument. If there are objections to the conclusions, appeals are allowed.

Voting – the following groups have the responsibility to vote and voting is compulsory.

Everyone over the age of 50.

Girls aged 10 and boys aged 11.

All 16-year-olds.

Adults aged 20-21, 30-31 and 40-41.

As mentioned earlier, everyone can debate (including these voters), but those listed above decide the policies. It is this ever-changing cross section of the population who take over from the career politicians of today. It may seem frivolous to suggest that children of ten and eleven should have to vote, but people of that age have a certain clarity of thought which should not be underestimated. It also teaches them how democracy works and the importance of their judgement.

There will be no political parties seeking power as is the case today, but people with shared interests can form groups and call themselves what they like. They can argue collectively or put forward a spokesperson – there is freedom of speech as there is today.

As you can see, the system is built on fairness where the power is spread to everyone and anyone who has an opinion on any matter. This is a democracy, remember.

The following is my suggestion for a manifesto which might be a starting point for the new system.

Housing

Everyone has a home. One home. As the state owns everything (this is communism, remember) there is no home ownership. No second or multiple ownership of property and no investment property (there is no investment). But everyone has a home – that is important. At the inception of the new system, no person or family will be turned out of their existing home and children can take over the family home on the death of their parents if that is their wish. Those who own more than one property must select the one they wish to live in.

February 2017 figures released show empty homes (UK) have doubled since 1996. 1.4 million empty and second homes at any one time in the UK.

It should be considered a basic human right to have a home and we all share a mutual responsibility to ensure that this happens. If individuals or groups wish to lead a life of travelling this will be supported.

Who gets a big house and who gets the one-bedroomed flat?

Films, the media and society in general depict a direct connection between wealth and grand properties – if you are rich you have a big house or many big houses. Property has to be maintained and managed. Without all the bragging rights what *is* a big house?

I hope that, under this system, people think more clearly and select the type of home which is best for them.

Housing is designated fairly and determined by need. Families would be allocated homes geared to their needs. Each case is decided on Its merits and the person involved will have a key say in the matter.

Bear in mind that this is merely a suggestion, as soon as the new regime is launched, policy is formed by parliament. But I would hope that home allocation will be decided on a needs basis and not by wealth or poverty as it is now. Because of the lack of commercialism, there will be no pressure urging folk to 'move up the property ladder'.

Education (work and retirement)

Education, work and retirement are linked here in order to illustrate how we might use our time. Formal education starts between the age 4 and 6 depending on the child. Education is a continuous lifelong process.

Under the current regime, education is primarily a preparation for a lifetime of work.

And although there are condescending channels to enable working class children to climb the ladder, the wealthy have one system and the poor have another. Education should be an end in itself, not a means to an end.

Work starts at around 8 or 10 years of age (just a few hours a week) depending on the child and never ends, there is no retirement (unless on health grounds) although hours worked will taper off as age increases.

Example – a 12 year old will be in full time education (2 or 3 days a week) but will be expected to work 2 or 3 hours a week. This work will be dependent on the child, his or her ambitions, strengths and weaknesses, but also on what work needs to be done. It is proper work and underlines the child's responsibility to society. As that person develops into his/her late teens, the work increases to, say, one day a week – early twenties two days a week.

During a person's periods of voting responsibility, work and study will be adjusted to take into account time spent on that task.

Because of the absence of money, it is anticipated that the full working week will be no more than 2 to 3 days. Currently around a third of the working population are employed full-time, in jobs which are exclusively associated with money, these people will be available for other work.

Work – by the late teens, early twenties a person may be aware of the path their main vocation will take - but what about the mundane, perhaps unpleasant tasks that need to be undertaken to ensure the smooth running of the community? Sewage plants, mortuaries, prisons, etc. have to be manned. Everyone has to take a turn doing these jobs, so a rota system will be established for everyone to take a share of the burden. It may be that some people are exempt from this – it would be daft to pull an eye surgeon out of the operating theatre to clear the drains – but at some time during that surgeon's life he/she would have cleared the drains, or something similar – you get my drift. I hope that in a new system like this, there will be room for common sense.

The way we view work/jobs will change. Work will be something that just has to be done in order that society functions – driving a train, filling a tooth, changing a fan belt, burying the dead – these are things which simply have to be done, done well and cheerfully, but let us not make a big thing about it. The idea that jobs have to be created to stimulate the economy and cheer up the chancellor will be redundant (as will the chancellor).

Back to education in more detail: from birth, each baby is observed by its parents and teams of specialists. The purpose of this is to discover the characteristics of the baby and, from an early stage, design a program of education tailor-made to that child. As the baby develops into a toddler, the program is fine-tuned and this continues as long as necessary. Any talents or special needs are taken into consideration. It could be that a child is athletically gifted and they may be interested in a path that will lead to sport. This will be encouraged. (Please note there will be strictly no interference or manipulation in the development of the child through its education path. The goal will be that the children develop in a way that leads them to being comfortable in their own skin, constantly challenged but comfortable. There is no question of tinkering to ensure fame or fortune.)

On the other hand, weaknesses will not be ignored, if a child has a blind spot when it comes to say, mathematics, help will be available, but not with the aim of ensuring success, some people just cannot grasp certain things and that is OK. Do not create anxiety by trying to change a person's core abilities. Look at what the child can do, and not so much at what they cannot do. If a nine-year-old cannot do sums, try again a year or two later. We are different, no one is 'normal', nor is anyone 'abnormal'. I'm almost certain that without the conditioning that occurs on the current education trail, we would all be defined as eccentric. It will not be the same education for everyone – for every hundred children, there will be a hundred tailor-made education tracks.

Education should inform and civilise, it should stimulate the child's imagination and challenge all facets of his or her creative potential.

Under the current regime, the above would be unthinkable due to the cost, but money does not exist and a surplus of workforce makes it possible.

The thrust behind my thinking here comes back to the duty we owe one another to enable each one of us to lead a fulfilled life, to have the time and resources to explore ourselves and develop into who we truly are without the constraints imposed by the need to earn money. Everyone can contribute most to society by being themselves, and by being fulfilled. There are dangers, of course, and I do not have all the answers.

As mentioned, a strong emphasis will be on creativity. Our creativity defines us and reflects who we are. Youngsters soak up facts, and they need that bank of knowledge, but even more important is establishing an environment where their creativity can flourish.

The focus will always be on what the child can do and who the child is. He or she may be gifted in art or music, or be mechanically minded, he or she may be funny, kind, sensitive and thoughtful, he or she may have a birth mark or impaired vision or they may be academic. Each and every child will be respected for his or her own worth and helped to take their place in society as a complete and unique individual and not categorised or pigeon-holed. To be happy and to contribute most to society, a person must have the confidence to be themselves, not to follow trends or be cowed by cynicism. Each child will have the best education, a unique education and an education that fits.

Class – we need to change the way we see each other and I hope that, under this new regime, class will disappear. So, no working class. No ruling class. No middle, upper or any other combination. No class. No rich no poor. No black no white. No gay no straight. Individuals, only individuals. I feel to classify a person is to insult them – the only label should be their name.

One of the most important jobs in society is parenting and so all parents will have as much time and (non-invasive) support as they need and other responsibilities will be limited.

Everyone works but they will also have the opportunity to study. A week will be, say, two days of work and one or two days of study depending on the person and their circumstances. It may be that those with a strong academic leaning will study three days and work one day. Or even a sabbatical of any length if this is desirable. There must be room for flexibility.

This is all fine in theory, but how does it function in practice? We are used to money. We work for it. We save it, spend it, borrow it, lie for it, steal it, kill for it. We envy those who have a lot of the stuff and look down our noses at those who have none. Some sell their bodies for it. We sing about money almost as much as we sing about love. What happens when suddenly there is none?

'Where do we obtain the things we need? Is everything free? Can we simply go to the supermarket and carry away the things we need? Can we go to the pub and drink away the evening without paying for the beer? And what about the jobs, why go to work if you are not going to get paid? I want a Ferrari – can I get one for free? I want a Picasso to hang in my living room'. And there is, of course, a significant difference between need and desire.

Let us take one question at a time.

Is everything free? No. You work for everything. Your work and your contribution to society gives you access to everything you need.

Example – a plumber spends two days a week plumbing. He needs a roofer, the roofer repairs his roof. He needs food, those working in the food industry provide food. He needs a dentist, the dentist fixes his teeth.

Example – the doctor needs an electrician. The electrician fixes his wires. The electrician gets a puncture in his van, the mechanic fixes the puncture.

I'm sure you get the point. It works pretty much the same as today, but no money changes hands. One subtle difference is our perception of each other – we are interdependent. The bus driver, the rat catcher, baker and the teacher all contribute to society and all benefit from society.

Can we take from the supermarket ad lib? Yes. There may be goods that are seasonal and there may be a scarcity of some items. A fair system of rationing will be developed in these cases. It will not be pricing that decides so that the rich benefit. There will be no rich or poor, nor will there be advertising to encourage consumption.

The pub and drinking all the beer, what about that one?

Yes and no.

Remember this is communism. The state owns everything and the people own the state and run it through a democratic system. Why does a landlord run a pub in today's world? For money. He dispenses alcohol (a toxin and depressant) for profit. I don't want to delve too much into the morality of drinking alcohol, but the image of the innocent, convivial local pub where friends meet for a pint or two might be examined more closely. But the people decide. If they want pubs and free beer that is up to them. The current regime turns a blind eye to the problems of alcohol, because it is a rich source of revenue through taxation.

Why work if you are not going to get paid?

I admit to finding this a difficult one but, on analysis, the doubts are of my fellow man and not the system. The change from a five-day to a two-day working week may be a great attraction initially, but a few decades on, when memories have faded – will it endure? The person who does not want to work has the power to put a question to parliament, there are no bosses, there are no unions – you are the boss – you are the government. There will be no buck-passing.

We all have an equal responsibility towards the system and if your question is – 'Why do I have to leave my warm bed on a cold winter's morning?' you are free to submit the question to parliament and wait for others to back you up, you might have to wait a long time. Even in a highly supportive and compassionate society, the individual has to exhibit a little backbone.

This new system, where there is no government as we know it, is based on trust and mutual compassion. Trust and compassion may be viewed as frail foundations on which to build a society ... or quite the opposite.

What about my Ferrari?

The traditional form of communism frowns upon such trophies of elitism and of course there are not enough Ferraris to go around. Why not build your own racing car? There will always be people who love cars, workshops and design facilities could be provided for them. Life should be about fun, not jealously guarding a status symbol. It could be made easy for those interested in fast cars to meet at a race track and drive such vehicles to their heart's content. There will be lots of leisure time, after all. There may be an arrangement whereby such activities could be awarded as recognition of an extraordinary deed or achievement. Parliament decides – you decide.

And that Picasso?

Works of art would be available at art galleries and museums.

***

Bear in mind that you are not voting for me or any smooth- talking megalomaniacal politician, you are voting for the right to decide. *You* are voting for *you*.

And if the majority vote for a return to the old Politics and an economy similar to the one we have today – that's what you'll get.

There is enough of everything to go around. The reason we want more is because consumption drives the economy and advertising drives consumption. I am sure we all think that we are strong-minded and not at all influenced by the advertising industry, but we succumb to their subtle jingles and flutter around the bright lights – we cannot escape. The economic hothouse has to be fuelled.

What about greed? Greed is a fascinating human trait and I wonder if, without the pressure from marketing and advertising, and with no fear of being left behind, it may become redundant or at least less common. I cannot change the way people are, nor do I want to change people, it is the system I want to change.

No one person can reconstruct an ancient and deep-seated culture that has evolved over thousands of years. This manifesto and the whole idea are nowhere near complete, nor is it ready to take over the management of any country. Some of the things I have not even touched on are – defence, royalty, international relations (and trade) and transport.

Leadership

There is no Prime Minister in this system, there are no ministers and no government as we know it and therefore no Prime Minister. In most modern democracies, people are accustomed to a figurehead of some sort. Perhaps a spokesperson could be nominated to perform that role. In a squad of rugby players, as the season plays out, leaders emerge without having been nominated as captains or vice-captains. It happens as personalities dovetail, it happens naturally without being forced.

Leaders will emerge, not to take over but to facilitate the appropriate landscape necessary in human interaction.

The day-to-day managing of the country will be conducted by what is now the civil service and their duty will be to ensure that there are enough man-hours available in the various sectors. The logistics will be complex to ensure, for example, that there is sufficient food in production and that it arrives at the table fresh and appetising. It is these logistics that will replace the current economy.

The form of direct democracy described here is not simple, nor is it without problems. If this system was incorporated right now – and due to a kaleidoscope of reasons such as the current education system, poverty and prejudice – many of those responsible for voting simply would not have the ability to make a balanced judgement.

The class system and the existing economic disparity ensure that the children of wealthy families are passed through the best schools and universities. I do not know, and this is partly speculation, but I believe coaching for leadership roles in government starts early within these establishments.

The reduction from a five-day to a two-day working week is an attraction only if everything else stays the same – which it will not, I am obliged to say. A poor man's life will improve significantly whereas a rich man will forgo privileges. The richer you are, the harder the changes are likely to be. Hard-working, self-made men and women will feel cheated of their wealth, they will disagree that wealth is futile and that time is more valuable than money. Nor will they appreciate that providing for their children financially will become unnecessary. But their day-to-day lives will not alter so dramatically, the main change will be not being able to view bank statements with high numbers in credit – their comfort blanket will be gone.

At the other end of the spectrum, a vast swath of the population exists that form a neglected section of British society. The current system has produced areas of industrial wastelands in the UK. Communities have been alienated by generations of poverty, there are middle-aged, unemployed adults whose parents have never worked due to economic changes.

It is this group of people whose circumstances would improve most under the new system. And, in turn, society will benefit from their contributions. It is a section of our society that needs compassion and they need to learn to accept that compassion. They deserve to have their lives back – to start again. Their children need to accept their parents and the parents need the chance to bond afresh with their children.

Example – just try to imagine a chap in his thirties or forties who maybe has children, he has been in and out of prison and he has never had a proper job. He is now free to express exactly what he wants out of life, free to explore his talents and free to talk about what really interests him. He no longer has to worry about survival, he has a home, warmth and nourishment. Would he like to study? Would he like to get fit and play football or wrestle? Would he like to go yachting or fishing or birdwatching? Perhaps he is dyslexic or maybe he has a mental health problem that has never been addressed.

Instead of being neglected, he now has the opportunity to do the things he wants to do; yes, he will have to work the mandatory two days a week, but only when he is fit and ready. Most people are innately good and kind when given the chance. This person is the victim of the current system where money has had priority over humanity for generations. He represents the deficit that needs to be balanced.

Another area that concerns me is the sex industry. Are all sex workers victims of their clients or are some of them happy, contented people? What will be their choice when there is no money? Will cases of rape increase if there are no sex workers?

***

Conclusions

I often reflect on the plight of the examples used at the beginning of this piece – of the little Brazilian boy, the mother living with her children in cardboard boxes, the spirit of the dead baby and even the hedge fund manager.

Gus Green, the little boy featured in my yet unfinished novel, 'The lives and deaths of Terry Toft' strikes up a friendship with Professor Rice, a professor of economic history. The boy is shocked when he learns that academics and historians of 2269 have concluded that money must have been a God – a ubiquitous God worshipped not only by individuals, but by all religions, nations and creeds.

It has been interesting studying counter arguments to my case regarding money, how in 3000 BC, early currency enabled trade to flow smoothly. The 'how many piglets in exchange for a goat? Or how many barrels of apples for a calf?' scenario is valid. *Was valid.*

Estimates of world population in 3000 BC vary between 14 million and 45 million. There were no apparent threats to the environment, unlike now with an expanding population of over 7.5 billion and frightening predictions for the future. Money is no longer the facilitator, it is no longer the means to an end – money has become the end itself.

As to my subordinate reason for writing this – to establish the root cause of why I have come to these conclusions – I still don't know, but to me it seems, with every passing day, even more clear and obvious.

Made in the USA
Las Vegas, NV
10 November 2021